Lesser Eternities

POEMS

Jim Glenn Thatcher

[signature: Jim Glenn Thatcher]

DEERBROOK EDITIONS

PUBLISHED BY

Deerbrook Editions
P.O. Box 542
Cumberland ME 04021
www.deerbrookeditions.com
www.issuu.com/deerbrookeditions

FIRST EDITION

ISBN: 978-0-9991062-2-8

Book design by Jeffrey Haste.

Contents

VI. Mantras From the Deep World

VII. Understory

To
Mickie,
Jeff and Charlessa Thatcher,

My longest friendships—
Rich Corozine
Don and Carol Kale

And to all my other friends
  Who've known me
    close enough to know
      That each line here
      Found itself
      As it rose
        Into meaning

I. Consciousness

The Spelling of Being

Early twilight . . .

The first few snow flakes
  waft down,
    slowly
      gently,
        into the woods;
each one large, luminous,
  shaped into its own
    individual character—
      solely its own, unlike any other
        since the beginning:
Each its own letter
  in the spelling of being;
    settling alone at first,
      then blending with
        its brethren as they fall,
too quickly,
  too thickly
    to be read
      if they could be read;
their meaning
  returning to its source
    in the alphabet of infinity;
their language universal
  but indecipherable,
    each character falling
      through its own encryption.

Evening descends.
  The snowfall thickens;
    inscrutable odes to mystery
      drift
        down
          through
            darkness. . . .

Interlinear

He sits in the darkness and watches the blizzard
and listens and thinks about language
while the wind whooshes and whispers and howls.
How words rise from our nature to make the world legible,
struggling toward meaning through the stutter of being;
through a gale of chaos and instinct and chance.

How the storm tonight is filling the woods
with a new page in its ancient encryption;
a swirling, shrouded, secret literature
that revises itself as it falls, obscuring every track,
every signature of life, in whirling drift;
spreading its hidden meanings
among the cuneiform scrolls of the birches.
Spruces sag under its portent.
The hemlocks stand their dark runes,
and each black twig in the scrub
is a character spelling its changing tale
in the white space forming around it.

By morning the storm will have gone.
He will go out under a blue and brilliant sky
to read the auguries of its passage in hieroglyphs
of shadow and light, ice and melt;
the ongoing translations of the text of the night
into that of the day, the ciphers of the thaw,
the always-decaying script of one moment
into the always-rising context of the next.

He will walk down the road to the field
by the water where new signs have formed,
passing from the instant of their imprint
into the history of the two hours since dawn:
The travels of two deer; a brief scatological
excerpt from the autobiography of a fox;
the fragment of a narrative of aging and hunger
in a hawk's fluttered and frustrated
strike in the snow.

He will be listening for the life of the day
all around him, straining to hear nature
reflecting upon itself in every stir of breeze
and drip of melt, every skitter of dead leaves
across the already crusting snow, every unseen
movement of flesh, each flicker of thought
rising through his own being.

He will be wondering what that fox hears
in what he hears now:
The endless epiphany of existence
in the calls welling world-ward
from a wheeling Babel of crows.

Gaia Dreaming

Tonight,
beyond this page,
beyond this lamp where I sit scrawling,
beyond the crickets trilling in the field,
beyond these woods, beyond the town,
beyond its lovers twining in their beds,
the blue-green earth is floating, all this upon it,
in a clear and cobalt darkness filled with scattered
incandescent worlds; a sensual, ripe,
imperfect paradise, like a voluptuous dreamer
lost in the mists of its longings.

The polar vastnesses sleep the slow grind of their glacial silence,
The tilt of their balance setting the opposition of seasons—
summer in north, winter in south—but the poles themselves
know only winter—the ice around them concealing dark waters
that surge with life—life in its legions swimming all the oceans
while the continents curl like lovers, yang to yin
in conjugal dance: Curve of Asia to the rump of Europe,
horn of Africa to the groin of Arabia, tongue of Sicily
to the toe of Italy, and the long licking reach
of Aleutia toward Kamchatka. The Nile's cleft oozes
the parted Rift of Africa, and the Americas are joined
like incestuous acrobats—below their isthmus umbilical
the vast cloacal womb of Amazonia and the Andes' spine
arching forever toward Asia, while across the roll and canyons
of the Pacific floor three thousand miles westward from
the precipice of Peru, scattered elements
of the spectral geography of South America
seem to reappear, strewn here and there
in random symmetry—submarine, somnambulant in the depths,
as though dreaming themselves as one—line for vague line,
range for random range, dilating in chthonic longing
toward the hot and feral haunch of Australia.

The breathing clouds billow with the breath of the planet
and all the life upon it—all the organic risen from the inorganic,
born from the earth itself, inherited through the chemistry of
Cosmos—
the subatomic seeds of life risen from stone---that stone
the bones of its body risen from the pulse of the magma
hemorrhaging from its heart— and below the stone, below
all else above, that magma floating continents through
eons of change and division, rupture and fracture
down the geology of ages; the rise of mountains, the gape
of gorges; the veins of the rivers changing their flow
with every change of the movement around them,
turning jungles into deserts, deserts into prairies,
prairies into forests, forests into jungles,
jungles into the next demand of circumstance
in the meander of Time, while around them all
the great ocean urge turns the slow wheeling
of libidinous eons in the endless circling welling
of her currents and streams, and down the great sea bottoms,
Atlantic and Pacific, in the deepest furrows of the deep,
longitudinal fissures swell and open in a continuous
orgasmic flow of red and molten lava, spreading
the globe unceasingly open, to drift and fold forever
back into itself in new and ever-changing forms—
matter enlivened into perpetual re-birthing,
almost organic in the flow of its changes;
a near-sentience asleep in the trance of becoming,
floating through an endless dreaming
of genesis and metamorphosis,
of fecundity and fire.

Notes from the Holocene

One summer I worked for geologists, drilling down
deep into glaciers and hauling up their histories
of ancient snows, layer by layer, change by change;
like tree rings, or the crushed and barren strata
of the frozen earth below: Here were the last seasons
of the mammoths, hunted into doom. And in these
few thin strata a narrow eon of bitter misery
that found its relief—of sorts—in the broad tan band
above—where algae briefly bloomed between
the blinding snows, and reindeer flowed
in broad brown rivers down the gravity of instinct
toward the memory of distant forage;
down where the haggard tribes had long since
scattered; following the terrain of visions,
the circumstances of hunger and chance.

And where I stood, above, in that blue and brilliant light,
I felt the lingering spectral presence of a vastness of ice
that in the mystery of its time had more than once
crushed and covered continents; harrowing mountains,
moving oceans, plowing seas where none had been before.
Destruction tilling creation down the long echo
of endless cataclysm; down through all
the warp of generations: Old worlds ever dying;
new worlds rising into being. Snows upon snows,
ice upon ice, generation upon generation,
adaptation upon adaptation, life upon death,
time upon time. A way, a wisdom building;
the mind of matter winding
through the weaving thrall of being.

Under the Sign of Kronos
—(March 6, 1988)

Tonight I stood outside and watched two planets
In a near-conjunction that will not occur again
For another thousand years: The bright slow glide
Of Venus and Jupiter; brilliant, steady;
Drawn together in a long-determined arc
Down the west and into the endless night
That always sleeps the circling world.

While over all Orion towered
Shining in the south, master of this night
Whose stars and galaxies knew more of time
Than any planet ever will. Watchful hunter,
Bow drawn back, aimed into the darkness
Of an eternity far beyond our own,
The time coming when his stars will have dispersed
Into another form—or forms—or formlessness—
Long after the passing of my kind,
Lovers of the same earth, the same light,
The same dream gone long into its night
When Orion hunts no more.

Later, behind closed lids, locked in the trance
Of meditation, I silently awaited
The conjuration of whatever was to come in the stars
Born visible from the vastnesses of my skull
And suddenly remembered the myth of Kronos,
Father of the gods, who rose from darkness
And devoured his children as they were born.

And then I saw great waves of flame billowing
As though from bright hot solar storms, sweeping out
To fall curling back upon themselves; great crescents
Licking endlessly at their own underbellies—
Great tear-drop orbs of fire—each ebbing
Its own shadow back into itself—its own demise,
Its own night, its own extinction. Toward that night
When Forever has burned itself away, and time
Has gone full circle, back to the sign of Kronos.

Lesser Eternities

The tragic beauty of mind—always leaning
toward meaning, but never finally reaching it.
"Infinity" we say, and find it too deep to fathom,
while "time" and "existence," which are within
and all around us, remain all too visibly invisible.

We inhabit an infinitesimal planet
on a wobbling elliptical orbit circling a star within a galaxy
within a fiery wheel of other galaxies,
all flinging ever outward into eons of endless emptiness.

And here, in the ever-changing moment
within this strangeness, everything is flux,
change and illusion of change:
Existence bears always the ghosts of its motion.
If this is all now in either ebb or flow,
who is to say and how would we know?
Time is time, and does not reveal itself.
Even place is not constant: Centuries, wars,
peoples, famine, floods—Ages great and dark
grow and fade, passing like ephemera over continents
that themselves pass through lesser eternities
around the world in perpetual geological drift.
"History" is what history does: the incessant welling
of present from past into the ever-erratic moment;
the word itself an unending argument of scholars
that only deepens the questions.

Meanwhile, from the still-cooling surface
of this at present semi-verdant skull of Earth,
consciousness rises slowly, in dim patches
—for how few millennia now?—
to blink in hungry atavistic wonder
at the discovery of itself—
drifting like tatters of fog through the forests of dawn,
posturing in the mirror of its ignorance.

Ice Night

On the first full night of astronomical Spring
Winter slept its deepest sleep,
Pregnant, heavy, glittering in its stillness
Under the great green vault of dancing Borealis.
A night so cold the mind withdrew into omniscience
And opened with the world outside.
Fur drew deeper in its lairs,
Neither owl nor fox could hunt,
And in the moonless, starlit brilliance
Deer stood struck through somnolent hours,
Their breath a ghostly silent sparkling fog.

Time itself seemed frozen into Presence—
An energy congealed, and taut with brittle tension.
No wind blew and no thing moved,
And only sound seemed living:
Old pines cracked like pistols in the woods, and
On the lakes the pressure of the ice reached crystal mass
To split against itself
          in lightning fissures cracking out
In cannonades across the compass of the dark,
To echo through the forests
And twang in pinging soundings
          down the muffled depths below,
Where lake trout sought the warmth of deeper waters,
To wait the rising-sooner dawns and dream
The fiery arch of summer's hall.

Spoor

As I lay waking this morning
my mind slowly revealed to me
the two halves of my brain
as the dawn - clear print
of a cloven deer hoof,
or two bear paws, side by side.

These two images
appeared in palimpsest succession;
one forming quietly
    over the other
        without disturbance,
           each equal to each,
and as they came to be there,
I felt the stirring
of some deep and totem thing within—
the gathering of darkness and light
into a powerful and sinuous form
not yet known to me,
coiling and uncoiling
throughout my being.

My nature is trying
to tell me something:
Inside I see a new snow,
fallen for clear and joyous tracking.

The Moon Thinks Brightly Tonight

The moon thinks brightly tonight. Sometimes it frowns a bit
behind thin nimbus, then spreads its halo in reassurance.
Reflects on the dim half of the world it shines upon. Wonders
why I'm walking this dark road with the black dog again. Frets,
worries a little. Wonders if I'm taking it seriously enough,
then once more smiles its radiance. Knows how many times
I've written of it; how many variations, with what love and awe.
Knows I'm imagining myself imagining this.

The black dog trots in the shadow line under the trees and smiles,
a dense vibrant invisibility moving on into the endless living moment.
I think of what I've just thought: "a dense vibrant invisibility
moving on into the endless living moment", and I am aware again
of the landscape that is always moving within me,
this hypnotic geography that dreams in my blood,
the oneness into which I long, body and mind,
to dissipate into, to become one with.

I open myself to this need, and the moon lays its light upon me
as grass, as aster, gentian, sweetfern, chicory of the soul as blue
as the sky—I become this headland and the tide-low sea around it,
become ice and water and this granite shelf and all the varieties
of sand into which time will grind it. Within and around me
I feel the movement of mole, owl, fox, mink, all the life in life
that wanders here tonight. I rise into white pine, red oak,
the darkness of hemlock, of spruce.

The moon dapples its shadow-wavering light onto the landscapes
of my interior, illumines the night Siberia of my soul,
where the tiger is one with moss-draped firs. I pass through tropics,
savannas, deserts, wandering toward the blue cliffs
of far-off mountains, my dreaming Abyssinias, range after range
retreating endlessly before me. I gaze over the curve of the horizon
toward the distant cities of day and night, and turn from them
toward solitude.

I pass alone and ghostly through the time-sweet silence of ruins:
through Tarquinia, sandy Pylos, Ephesos, high Mycenae
of the lion gate, the rose-grey Petra of night, then re-emerge
half a world beyond them, staring outward from the black
and sightless windows of an abandoned cliff dwelling
up under a canyon rim. The low moon glints in my eye
through every opening, reflecting back upon itself
and then down upon me here, filling me with its grace,
its dumb understanding.

I keep to the dark road, walking fast, joyous; every molecule open
to a vast and immediate mystery; answer the depth
of an owl's call with the depth of my listening, look upward again
and the moon guides my gaze beyond itself, into the depths,
the long, far depths of this beautiful, now cloudless night.

Consciousness

"Full moon," he murmurs: Stealing its light from the unseen sun.
Sparkling the snow, shadowing the woods, whitening the reach
of the rolling fields, almost extinguishing even Orion.
He is alert. Thinking about his thoughts and watching the road ahead
for the sudden leap of a deer that could end them forever,
their random preciousness gone without recall or value
into the empty clarity of the air—its invisibility already filled
with an unheard human cacophony—radio, cell phones,
high-speed coding: opera, rock, hillbilly, arguing lovers,
the full-tilt runaway di-di-di-dahs of latter day digital Morse—
all of them lost in their turn, their energy swirling on into
a universe of constantly shifting forms.

The road curls through curves across long open meadows and up
along their shadowed skein of trees—spruce, hemlock, white pine,
red oak, birch, beech, aspen. Proud that he knows them even in
the speeding darkness. Senses again the oneness of things—
his being one mind in a history of billions; given life by
the stars, risen from the dust of this now strange planet
into a species with an unknowable destiny, gifted with intelligence
but hindered by its weaknesses.—Thinks about the lights
in those houses by the water a half-mile ahead, then about
lights in houses beyond that water, and the minds within those
houses, each of them unique, thinking in its own untranslatable
exactness of Icelandic, Danish, French, German, Finnish, Russian.

Thinks about the fragility and the resilience of those minds,
but mostly their fragility. About his own gifts and failings—
the slow gain in the losses, the slow growth through the wastes.
He smiles at the joy of being an infinitesimal speck
in the world's mystery, his smallness in these fields,
one glittering sparkle in its moment in an eternity of snow,
finally triumphant for having lived at all.

II. Finding the Way

Exile

Always the longing. Six years old in West Virginia
and hating it. His father long gone into the Pacific war;
heroic, Odyssean, loved fiercely but barely remembered.
Every Fall, his mother dragging him from home, Demeter-like;
from the Adirondacks into this underworld
peopled by her kin. Dead brown hills strip-mined
to the shale. Roads paved with cinder.
The rivers thick, viscous, sulfuric with yellow mud.
The sky filled with coal dust; towns grimed with it,
snow blackening as it fell, the smell of darkness
filling damp winter daylight. His grandmother's house;
next door, the brick district school building—mean,
looming, smelling of sour milk and passing skunk.
Miss Shreve the first grade teacher; towering, red-faced, shrill.
Shrieking that he had no imagination because he saw a
picture in a way other than the way she wanted them to see it.
Across the alley the drunken blacksmith who looked like Hitler,
cursing, hammer and anvil ringing with rage as he
shod horses, endlessly blinding the iron-red eye
of his life in the hissing steam of his cauldron.

Listening in bed at night to coal trains two miles long
straining through the valleys, locomotives building steam
in the yearning distance. Building and chugging.
Wanting to ride into that long darkness with them,
steel on steel, driving wheels sliding silvery
on the dark rails; to ride through the universe
of night and wake to Spring in his father's country:
pine mountains, granite cliffs, the sky always blue,
the lake in bright sunlight, its hundred islands
become the continents of his dreaming world.

Sonnet of the Drunken Son

My father died on Christmas day
When I was nine and filled with magic,
And left his haunted drunken spirits
Wandering in my drunk-mad soul.

Left the haunting of his passage,
Left delusions of his meaning,
Left the dream of heroes tragic,
Reeling in my drunk-mad soul.

And left my loyalty in his ways,
Left his anger down my days,
Howling in my drunk-mad soul.
Left his legacy in my madness;

My cup his long-forgotten, buried sadness
Raging in my drunk-mad soul.

Stray

I have lost my taste for authenticity.
Sometimes passing the mirror of a strange window
I am haunted by the old man with eyes like the sadness
of a summer ocean, who camped every year
along the abandoned road to the village.
I used to pilfer the family larder for him,
straining even then to create the tragedy
I believed worthy of my destiny.

He was a disappointment, but I have followed my mythos.
Once on a freighter I peeled potatoes,
the small knife they had issued me curling off
my spiralling ticket from one continent to another.
Everything since then has gone as it would.

I drive through the heartless dream
of an endless winter morning.
I have forgotten place. My vows have taken me,
the marrow soul of an old car flailed by crosswinds.
Somehow it is always March, the wind lashing me
with its whip of indecision. The roads always dirt.
The sky a blue hammer.

A landscape that changes only in its particulars.
Everything under the ominous sun
filled with stubbled fields, the skeletal shadows of trees;
the constant brittle threat of cold and dissolution
mitigated only by the dry savor of abstraction,
a dream of absence, of disappearance
into an empty geography.

In Circleville

In Circleville the mountains' shadow never lifts—
not for the sons sprung like doomed lambs
from the warm womb onto a barren hearth
on the cold earth of a black day in wet spring.
They have entered the realm of their heritage.
They will dwell in the shadow and envy the light.
They will be seekers, suspended in the web of indecision
that sways in the breath between heaven and earth,
their souls bare and brittle as the souls that sired them.

The daughters, their sisters, are grim and heartless,
embittered by the betrayal of their brothers' lost causes.
The fathers die young and swim in the dead light of lost planets.
Their deaths are the legends their sons yearn to live.
The mothers—ah, the mothers. They are the daughters also of
                                                    mothers.
They have become angels wicked in their righteousness.

But think of the sons, who must wander helplessly
the feral strangeness of their destinies,
who must ride always onto the field of honor between
the world within and the world without,
who must die for the fathers within them.

Think of the bleak winters streaked with desolate light,
the grim-rimed nights of alcohol and treachery,
the incessant obsession with suicide,
the pistols in the mouths, the murders real and imagined,
the self-fulfilling prophecies.

Think of the silent hate around the mouths of the women,
the cold beds bitter with dread and denial, the spell cast and molded
even in the sons in the seed of the sons as they piteously
dream themselves riding forward into the dark light,
trembling in their dread and eagerness.

Not in This City

The city sleeps here by the tide that he is still unused to,
but he does not. He dreams awake through the short summer nights,
gulls wheeling in eerie clouds underlit by street lamps,
fish swimming through his open windows; mackerel, hake,
haddock, schooling down from the grey pre-dawn depths
below Arcturus and Jupiter.

The illuminated falsely Georgian Greco-Roman levitating piers
of the Playskool parking garage ascend into the night
like cosmic ice-cube trays. Across the way lurks the dark
ambivalent emptiness of the yellow brick Lubyanka High School,
the blackness of its doors leading into a deeper, more sinister, night;
the dread beckoning of misplaced memory a dim glow waiting
down the far reaches of its corridors.

In the little park below his window five copper figures
representing "Ascent" climb a small stone pyramid. In the dark, alive
and mischievous, scrambling and whispering in their night-games,
they appear to him as succubi, their delerial sexuality wet, tumescent,
open and gaping, male and female waxing and waning
with the hours of the night.

Two stone Han sages in the gardens of the library roof
face each other in perpetual greeting. He imagines himself
there with them, seated on a wooden bench under the classic yew,
rooted in marble, serenely eroding in the acid rain.

At last he enters into sleep, lets the vision take him, finds surcease
in dream. Not in this city, a voice tells him. Then its echo.
Not in this city. Something holds its breath, denies, conceals itself,
but there's only a flurry of brown leaves whirling across
the downdraft plazas. Seasons passing seasons, voices in the rain,
whispering in the wind, snow swirling into a cold blankness
that envelops him in whiteness, a bitter softness fading into warmth.

Beyond Even Lethe

A fallen student of history
Filled with divine amnesia,
I entered Rome through a sea of wine,
Swam like a fish through the arch of Hadrian,
Suckled the teat of the Etruscan wolf
Beloved of Rumina, the goddess of memory
Before drifting on down with the ethereal stream,
Lost in a trance of *kif* and *retsina* ,
Adrift in the fluids of time and forgetting,
Tumbling the currents of desire and delusion,
Cursed by the singing of Calypso and Circe,
Ebbing and flowing into the tides of creation;
Following the Bull into the birth-giving sea,
Leaping with dolphins over the belly of Europa,
Flowing for eons down the long sweeping currents
Back into Egypt and up through her silt,
Struggling her eddies with the blindness of sturgeon,
Pulsing the soul of the swift-flowing stream
Beyond the cities of Karnak and Thebes,
Beyond the cataracts of knowing and belief,
Beyond the abilities of magicians and priests,
Beyond the lands of mystery and genesis,
Beyond even Lethe and the waters of memory,
Into the reaches of darkness and dreaming,
Waiting the starlight and waiting the dawn,
An eternal narcosis, an endless suspension,
Always becoming and always receding,
Always receding and always becoming,
Always and forever becoming
and receding.

Ambulatory Under Heaven

As soon as pen touches paper
I have everything and nothing to say.
How many years? The emblem has faded.
Our last visitation was ephemeral.
Lost in wine the train climbing slowly
over Brenner Pass. The dim compartment
and the moon on snow.
Once again we were both reading Dostoevsky.
A solitary pleasure with the risk
of grave social consequences.
Now even to think of you I reproach myself.
In this you have become part of me.
Otherwise much has changed. I am re-learning
to breathe. I have not succeeded
in abandoning literature.
It falls from me like over-ripened fruit
and rots on the ground around me.
I am a dying orchard ambulatory under heaven,
a future of fallow permutations.

What if I lied, giving you only
the truth that I aspired to?
What if I told you I was happy?
That I have stepped away from history?
That I dream of a lake the bottomless
depth of forgetfulness. What then?
Would I have earned your contempt
or have you too embraced your complexities?
Would you flee in feigned horror?
Turn from the light sparkling the blue waves?
I have seen how you have known the river only,
in its silt the soft faces of drowned philosophers.
How it flows through a wilderness
of lost possibilities toward an ever-receding
horizon, and from this distance
I imagine you obscured in a mist of thin rain,
drifting always away, lost
in a paradise of invisible years.

Fossil Light

After a long parting, we were once more watching the stars.
Always as though they could tell us
something of their meaning and our own.
But what do we know of the language of light?
Of its silent passage through millions of years?
You said you wanted to rise with me again
into the stream of the Zodiac, remembering
those many nights long ago when we'd stood
in that old field staring skyward toward the planets
and formations we could name and then on into
the unknown swirls of stars and galaxies
beyond them, as far as our vision could reach.
          As though all rifts were not immense.
As though we could drift the raft of Scorpio
on its sidereal glide down the unending West.
As though its stars were intimate objects,
luminous pulsations in the constellations of our bodies,
at no greater distance than the darkness
between attraction and choice.
          But for me it was too late:
The gravity of the small dark planet within me
held me back; a collapsing weight heavier than light
in the regions of my solar plexus.
If memory holds truth, it is only in specimen,
a fractal entrance into a perceived occurrence,
the cross-section of a moment
like those cutaway views in the illustrations of my boyhood:
The pilot in the cockpit, the captain at the periscope;
neither in their own element nor mine.
But I peered in at them as though
I peered through the page,
lured by the suggestion of the real,
a metaphor so obvious I didn't see that it was metaphor.
          Like the stars. Their presences that are not present,
but images from the past, the play of fossil light
vibrating in the retina, translating softly
through our quivering cells.

Finding the Way

The stark pall of still another late November;
grey half-light on dim-shadowed snow,
skeletal trees leaching black veins into a dead sky.
He's surprised that now he sees the beauty
in this darkness, when before it had meant only
raw misery; a deep dread of the bitter months
ahead and a longing for the golden green of August,
the time he's always loved and never wants to leave.
These past few years there's been another element—
he knows he's older than he wants to be, knows
the endless cycle of the seasons can only
be counted on until his own counting is over;
that he might not see another summer.

When he thinks of that, the old shroud falls
over him again—takes him back to that longest
dark season of his life—all those years of hibernation
in alcohol; dormant, helpless, dreaming toward the light.
Decades of living the novel but never getting it past notes—
thousands upon thousands of words flung onto their pages
but never building the book.—Suddenly he catches himself—
realizes he's doing it again—mourning the irredeemable,
creating nothing but more nothing—turns back
to the poem, hurls himself onto it—becomes the page itself;
gets *this* line down, lets it take him where it will,
then *this* line—alive again in the fury of becoming—
forgetting fate, finding the way.

The Drunken Novel

Himself the novel wanting to be its novelist.
Living it, suffering it, writing it, but never building the book.
Derelict words by a drunken writer in a staggering scrawl
across one first page endlessly abandoned to another.
The beginning unending and never beginning.
The protagonist become his own incessant antagonist—
gifted in words but lost in discipline.—The pages delirious,
stumbling, wandering—nothing but notes, fragments, para-
graphs—
some brilliant, but none settling into a story—its idea elusive,
ever-changing.—Every moment another metaphor,
every day another allegory—their meanings his meanings
but overwhelmed and entangled, dragging him down
into the ever-darkening maze.—Beer blackening his being.—
His own first person anguishing in its poisoning—
all day every day through all those years
every cell in his body screaming in withdrawal—
all night every night drunk again; the agon of agony
from that dark attic in Bethlehem through all the ensuing hovels
and rubbles, all the labor and factory jobs that followed.
Physical addiction validated by moral obligation—
He thought he needed suffering— The Authenticity of Tragedy—
Was he not living it? The Sisyphus of Six-packs?
The Tortured Hero proud to be deluded in his delusions?—
The Great Novel of the Western World?—To someday
be recognized as worthy of his tradition—Dostoevsky,
Hesse, Knut Hamsun, Conrad, Kafka, *Heinrich Muller*—
Apostates all, attitudes and atmospheres matching his own wan-
derings—
That negative apartment on Positively 4th Street—cockroaches
swimming in his tea, crawling through his rice....
The abandoned MA thesis—Freud and the Philosophy of History,
itself evaporating before the novel, undone, studied but not written,
obsessed over—pages begun and fallen away, adrift
in the litter of the lost literature of his own lost lifetime.
Years and scrawlings carrying him on, sketching his situations—

the Time Farm in Pennsylvania— Settled there by old friends.
Like him, all ex-history students. Horses, guns, drugs. Stoned.
Riding out into the fields of night, each in his own century—
his the 19th—Russia—*Holy Mother Russ*—then back every day
to his job in the hangover factory.—The year in Greece—
The lover of ruins ruined himself and knowing it.
Astray across Crete, angst in every pen scratch. Then coming
back to hole up for three winters in that abandoned farm
outside of Circleville, what was left of the house slowly
caving in around him. Snakes in summer sliding up
between the floorboards, winter coming in through the holes.
The pen hapless in his hand. Decades pass, the novel long dead,
entombed in the marbled covers of abandoned notebooks—

Let them lie there. That history now his strength.
His life still literature. He has risen from regret.
The 'fragments' he now writes not fragments but poems—
They carry their full meaning.

III. One Among Many

Negative Capability

"...that is when man is capable of being in uncertainties,
    Mysteries, doubts without any irritable reaching after fact
        & reason." — John Keats

He's reading Gilgamesh again:
Navigating his way back to the beginnings;
back upstream, seeking the source.
Opening himself to the current—
letting it flow through him, his body and mind
becoming its world completely.—
The feral companion born of the wilderness;
the ordeal in the Cedar Forest;
the despairing search for immortality
in the marshes at the edge of the world;
then the narrative itself trailing off, fading out,
sinking into lost millennia;
disappearing and forgotten,
to rise again from clay shards
into this century, this moment, his hand, his eye....

So much of his life given over this way
Mapping the human; seeking the source.
The Deep Lives, he calls them, real and imagined,
myth, fact, and fiction welling from their depths,
made larger by the way they were lived
and the passions that wrote them down.
The many-mirrored facets of the self
and its self-contained opposites. Homer,
Beowulf, the Grail myths, Cervantes, Tolstoy—
Strindberg and his romance with madness,
Dostoevsky the Everyman of extremity,
Quixote following Parsifal as the fool on his quest.

He turns to the dead as they had turned to each other,
to understand the living. Learning who he is
and sometimes who he is not, then learning
to live with that. He thinks of Keats calling Balboa
Cortez and not caring, then smiles to himself,
puts down the book and looks out at the stars:
thinks how he keeps re-learning the constellations,

season after season. Like the ancients. Searching
for something that can sometimes be found, but never kept.
Open to the night and all the names of the un-nameable.

Mystery Incarnate

The Neanderthal and Buddha, algae and Christ,
the gnats in the palace at Knossos, the mosquito
at the blood of the Maya. We try to look into our nature
and are confounded, searching for the force in matter
that binds us with all. The animal that
sustains us bounding within, the mineral rising
from earth to blood, the vegetable that feeds us
life like our own. The long rise from nothing
to fire to stone to ocean to life to land,
protoplasm into thinking biped vertebrate:
the *mutatis mutandis* of transformation,
metamorphosing down from Lascaux
through Ovid through Darwin through
Dawkins, Wilson and Gould.

Cut into us and we are flesh. Blood and liquids streaming.
Gristle, muscle, membrane, fat, bone and marrow,
the mysterious pulse connecting an animate all.
Magnify the image and we are cells and structure;
tubes, tunnels, underworlds of forbidden cities.
Focus in and we open into labyrinths and galaxies
of molecules and atoms, the beauty in the sleep
of a dreaming Galileo.

The closer we come to it the grander the metaphor.
All of this taken in by the incessantly murmuring mind,
itself an elusive presence. "Brain," we call it, and include
the body. "Heart" and "spirit" and none suffice.
Some look deeper. Recognize the impossibility and
embrace it. Knowing that their knowing is only ignorance
given fancy. But go on anyway, wanting to believe
that what they do is the truest of the truly human.

Haunted by the unfamiliar familiarity of faces on the street,
risen through the slow building of the legions behind us:
Celt, Pict, Saxon, Magyar, Tartar, Han, Nubian,
Athabascan. We look outside to see the inside. Delve for
their mysteries and find mostly our own. A glimpse
of Attila at the edge of the crowd, Falstaff farting at the bar,
a wink from the smiling Etruscan.

Art and ruins, mythos and mystery, psyche and soma,
genome and meme. Fragments of fragments,
translations of translations. We find their poems,
scan their lines to feel their knowing, study their art
to see their world, strain for their voices through
the delusions of distance. Sappho and Sophocles,
Bhagavad Gita, Song of Solomon, Lao Tzu, Li Po,
Basho, Dante, Quixote. The undying epic of the likeness
within us, Gilgamesh to Odysseus as Ulysses twice over.
What they have given us best are gifts of self
and longing—bright flashing moments
when brief shimmers of meaning leap like salmon
above the currents of our unknowing.

One Among Many

Athens, Vassiliseis Sofias Avenue

As from a great height
I see myself
Below—alone, anonymous—
Struggling through the tangled currents
Of a great multitude
On the wide modern boulevard
Of an ancient city,
Under a thin filigree of leaves
In the vast transcendent brightness
Of an eternal autumn afternoon.

Suddenly—
Despite myself—
From the deepest center of my being,
I feel the urgent, inexorable rise
Of a teeming procession of spectral humanity,
Endless, uncontainable in its stream,
Welling up through ten thousand years
And the infinite distances of the mystery within,
To carry this fluid moment forward
Into a future
Far beyond
My own.

Philosophy and Osracism; Athens, 1975

The last time we argued, Zeno—
Old Double-tongue*—
Down in that bar on the Street of Smiths
Where the subway briefly rises
Then runs again to ground
Under the temple of Hephaistos—
You conjured yourself out of infinitude
And the depths of my stupor,
And were pounding the table,
Slopping my wine all over the zinc.
As real as you could ever be,
You tedious bastard—
Ever since grade school
I'd wanted your throat.

But when the shouting began
It was me they came after:
An enraged taverna-keeper
And six "noble" Athenians,
To throw me contemptuously
Into the gutter;
A derelict drunken foreigner
Screaming into nothingness—

How were they to have known
That I was a man
Gifted
In paradox?

The epithet given by his contemporaries to Zeno of Elea (c.490-c.450
BCE), Zeno the philosopher of paradoxical mathematics. (See endnotes)

To Old Yuan Chi,* A fond Reply

> In morals I was greater than Yen and Ming.
> Always I gazed from the window in all directions;
> I climbed up mountains to greet what I so piously expected.
> All I saw were tombs and mounds on the hills.
> Ten thousand ages passed in a single moment...
>   —Yuan Chi, "Speaking My Mind"

For years I studied history, philosophy, and literature,
Pursuing the past for a key to my destiny.
At twenty-one, when I found my first poem by you,
It was already the story of my life.
From behind a grim visage I despised my own times;
Detested this century and everything within it.
Armed thus with my anger,
I then set out to nurture my sufferings—
To strengthen my belligerence—
To buttress my despair.
The decades that followed were an orgy
Of wine and deprecation, of bitterness and folly.

All to no avail: Nothing changed but my mind.
One day I awoke to find myself wearied of this weariness,
This conflict with conflict—saw that
The world was a joke I'd played on myself.
Once I had seen this, everything changed:
I surrendered to the laughter within my sadness,
Abandoned cause in favor of effect,
Ceased to carry an ax to banquets.
Since then my gratitude is boundless:
I am happy to be here, fully alive in this summer night—
Watching these fireflies, writing this poem,
Thinking of you.

*Yuan Chi (210-263C.E.), a scholar-poet born in Honan (see endnotes).

"Poor Old Sodden Li Po?"

The old tales tell how, after years of libation,
Li Po* drowned one night while trying to embrace
The moonlight undulating on the river.
And there his biography ends,
As though that moonlit water
Merely bore him off into legend.

But what if it wasn't true?
What if, after all those years of romancing his wine
The old poet ended up all wet in other ways as well?—
First in his body, then in his brain,
And finally in the myth of his life?
What if old Li had been too drunk
In those last years
to have written any poetry at all?

What if his root-tangled body had been found
By some honest old boatman in three fingers of water
Not two feet from where he had fallen?
What if there were no "depth" to the story at all?
What if old Li's "drowning" could be less
Romantically described as a "fatal gargling"?

And what if, for the rest of his own life, that old boatman
Had been literate enough—and gifted—and sober enough—
To fill his solitude by imagining himself
Some drunken poet named Li Po?

What then? "Li Po" would not have been Li Po,
But the poems would still have been "his" poems,
And the traditions, (which become "history"),
Would have lied again. Alas, how often
Can Beauty be trusted to follow Truth?

*Tang Dynasty, 8th Century. (see endnotes)

50

More Like Poor Old Tu Fu
—after Sam Hamill

One hot August day on a mountaintop,
after many years parting,

Li Po met his old friend Tu Fu,*
and found him sad, wan, exhausted.

"Poor old Tu Fu," he thought,
"must be agonizing over poetry again."

When I was a young student,
I thought myself like Li Po—

Free, wild, and wanton—
in life and in writing.

But now, all these years later,
I see I've always been more like poor old Tu Fu:

Still agonizing over life—
Still agonizing over literature.

*Tang Dynasty, 8th Century. (see endnotes)

Bittersweet

Fog and rain. October leaves
luminescent; red, orange and yellow
in the wet grey air. I've been on my job
in the woods, clearing Asian bittersweet,
week after week—hacking, snipping,
sawing, pulling it up by the roots,
and I've just given up for this day,
had enough, and come back to my car.
I'm wet, and so are Li Po and Tu Fu,*
right here beside me as always,
uncomplaining, enduring it all
in Taoist silence. We have known
many rains together; me driving,
they resting here in the car door pocket,
their pages long since stained and warped—
as befits the millennium between us—
by window-leaking weather.

Poems luminous as these wet autumn leaves,
written by two friends wandering
great distances apart—messages that
each knew the other might never see,
in a country fragmented by war,
drought, fire and famine—its factions
entangling; strangling each other
like these vines I've been battling,
which came here from there—all these
centuries later—to overwhelm oaks,
pull down these pines, give me this work,
this bittersweet metaphor –these two poets
drifting down the endless river of time
through ages no less tragic than their own
into these wet woods, this old car—
their words still seeking each other,
their lives flowing into mine.
*8th Century. (see endnotes)

The Ten Thousand Tears

Jyou Bu-Zhen was a brilliant poet, some said,
But a lazy one. Others saw a method in his idleness.
This was not sloth, they held, but an element of his gift.
Poems came to him like butterflies to a flower.
They left their pollen in his ear, then flitted off again
Into forgetfulness. They fluttered to him in his dreams,
And while he walked, and when he sat down with his bowl,
And even as he begged his way from village to village.
But Bu-Zhen never wrote them down.
He would recite them as they came, then let them
fly off again, he said, back to their nature.

A poet with no poems. Yet he had disciples.
(Who can account for these things?)
They pleaded with him to write them down,
But he refused, nor would he let others
Write them for him. "Would you deprive
The bees of their nectar, the flowers of their life?
Spring comes, then Fall. Life is not lost in Winter.
When I am gone, find my poems in your grains of rice."

When old Bu-Zhen died, they cried for him,
And in each tear, they said, grew a tiny chrysalis
And from each chrysalis grew a butterfly,
And from each butterfly a single poem flew.

Crossing Spruce Mountain, Thinking of Bashō *

White pines like
great Buddhas rising softly
through the fog.

The mountain road
winding toward its narrow
misty pass.

Each blurred ledge,
each ghostly hemlock,
like brush strokes

on a gray scroll,
unfurling down from your time
into mine;

this slow poem
forming quietly
through the wipers

*Matsuo Bashō, 1644-1694 (see endnotes)

To the Bronze Lady of Xanthos Found in the Deep, this Fragment, Too Late, from My Loss

In my dreams
I would have navigated the stars
to have found you,
would have sailed night's heavens
as well as its seas,
full rudder deep and steady;
would have held the silent wind
in pure sails, tiller taut
toward my quiet courage;
would have felt the balm of vast night
all around me,
to ache through my watch
for the touch of your belly.

And all the while knowing
that on the slow voyage
through the trial of my longing,
I faced no greater peril
than the despair
of an endless desire;
no sweeter promise
than the copper bitterness
at the crux of your thighs;
no greater distance
than the teeming centuries
between your time
and mine;
no greater failure
than waking
to morning. . . .

The Last Dream of Henri Rousseau*

Gathering vagrant forms from the black vastness
of a deep sleep, an awareness rising,
dimly at first, before willing itself into clear lucidity
as his mind opens slowly from the barren sands
as though from the dome at Palomar
onto a pale full moon fixed blank and omniscient
over desert rocks crouched like gnomes—
short, squat, upright, strange—
guarding the sleeping pool
where wolves crouch petrified in living stone
and the fire is hours dead
the hours dead like centuries,
the lion lain down by the sleeping gypsy
under the beacon palms, waiting
for other travelers in strange garb,
faces drawn as though by the hand of a child,
destinies frozen in still life. . . .

And all the while, overhead,
in the silent slow-motion somnolence
of this unending night,
the red stars exploding soundlessly,
shimmering translucent confetti
from the next eternity into this.
Waiting for the next moon,
and the next sun that never comes;
only this pool and this moon
and the red starlets
in their multitudes,
illumined in a black
and unfathomable sky.

* French Post-Impressionist painter

IV. Sanding Blue Doors

Adjunct

Freshman English. First day of new term.
He walks into the room. A required course.
Staring students; some friendly, some leering,
whispering to each other. Some, he knows,
semi-literate, feeling like prisoners—
filled with fear of this long-hated subject.
All of them taking him in: disheveled hair, beard,
work shirt. Definitely not their vision of an "academic"—
a word he doubts that half of them have ever heard
in this simple context—a "college teacher".
The holes in the left knee of his jeans
are not fashion statements—He does field work
to back up his $1,965 per course "professor's" pay—
Last week he was clearing brush, burning stumps,
then putting it all into a poem. A few days before
that he was painting a fence and doing the same.

This term he carries two sections of this course—
all to back up his love of Lit—the reason he's here.
If it weren't for that, he'd have left long ago—
slammed the door on American Academe,
that very Temple on the Hill of hypocrisy—
deceitful Upholder of Civilization and its Values—
now fallen into the true "values" of that "civilization"—
the push for profit and power—callous exploiter
of the dreams and ambitions of students—and
of his—and thousands of other adjuncts—love
of their subjects more than their pay.

He puts down his books and looks out at the class.
As unhappy about teaching it as they are about taking it.
He smiles at the irony. Literature is lived.
He takes the roll. Lays down the laws.
Tells them that all learning is learned by the Self.
They have to want it.

Now—let us open the book and begin—

Sanding Blue Doors

This morning I'm sanding blue office doors, doors so blue
they could be a passage into deep afternoon. I start at the top,
moving the sandpaper straight up and down, and am surprised
when under my fingers clouds begin to form; long streaks
of cirrus at first, and then, just as I begin to sense my power,
I remember that cirrus means rain the next day,
and tomorrow's my day off.
I change the forecast by smoothing my stroke to a wide irregular roll.
There's a new front coming through, cirrus giving way to nimbus—
I can afford the magnanimous gesture of a few transitional showers
before I apply the broader, wider, more generous strokes of cumulus.
Suddenly an hour's gone by and I realize I've forgotten myself.
How many secretaries have stepped quietly by my oblivion
without noticing these soaring Turneresque sandpaper skyscapes
that have turned both sides of both stairwell doors
into great back-to-back flawed mirrors of the heavens?

Behind the clouds the blue is getting darker,
and I search its recesses for the first stars, conjuring them by desire:
Arcturus in Bootes; Jupiter leading the path of Sagittarius;
Antares, the pulsing heart of Scorpio. With the touch of a finger
I place them in their proper alignments, and, prospering,
take my place as the gigantic astronomer in a medieval woodcut—
feet on the earth, head and shoulders projecting through
the firmament and into the spheres beyond.

Now for the arch and vault of the elevator entrance.
I drag over the ladder, scour clouds across the overhead
and let thunderheads roll down the insides of the frame.
A Pacific depression roils across the vast expanse of
the wide-jawed doors, then dissipates into paradisal cottony puffs
scattering pleasantly through azure tropical distances.

Nothing left but the inside edges!
I brace the doors open with both feet, and with my one free hand
struggle with the laws of physics! At last they catch open!
I have parted the heavens! I have spent an entire morning working
in the full power of my imagination. I have discovered
a new medium and in the process will probably have pleased
my employer, who is going to pay for all this in ignorance
of the prodigious service he has performed for art and cosmos.
He's a busy and generous man, bless his heart,
who thinks he's my boss, and not my patron,
who I can be sure hasn't checked the weather all morning
and who never wants to be bothered with details.

Blue-Grey Fence—Imagined Museum of Imgined Art

It's a blue-grey day, the sky sulking undecidedly against itself
and I've just been handed two gallon cans of blue-grey paint
and a five-inch brush to slather a three-sided fence—
more like a stockade, really—vertical boards over six feet high
topped by a foot high lattice—to enclose gas tanks
and other equipment behind a meeting house. A blue-grey day
with blue-grey pay and I want something more than this—
I want Art.—Art with a capital "A"— To turn this paint job
into Art itself—To take the reality of this fence and outdo it—
Create it anew into a concept beyond "realism"—I'll call it
"Meta-realism"--a reality true to the dreaming artist
in my own inner self . . . I open the first can. Stir the contents.
Ready myself. Dip the brush. No longer a fence I face,
but an easel. I slap the color on—thick—smooth. . . .
Saturate the wood beyond the wood that I'm saturating—
recreating the fence itself into something other than itself.
I go beyond painting into sculpture. Beyond sculpture into
non-dimensional three-dimensional creation. My hand paints
the fence; my mind takes it, reshapes it. The lattice turns to
a geometric Chinese design then fades, disappears completely
and I change the color of the wall beneath to bark brown at first—
the upright planks become the log walls of a frontier fort—
but that's not what I want—it's only a start—a rite of passage,
and now the blue returns, bluer and bluer with every slurp
until the grey is gone and the day more free and the boards blend
into a singular surface flowing into an endless canvas upon which
appear an endless succession of images changing and changing
from the blue of Turner's skies and oceans into the darkness of
torch-lit cave walls filled with the brilliantly primitive outlines
of prehistoric bison, deer, the bulbously-buttocked goddesses
of the paleolithic and then the light grows again, rising and falling
through the days and nights of eons and the art of each epoch—
the sideward-peering eyes and spread shoulders of Egyptian tombs;
the abstract linear images—all cones and circles and squares
of Gilgamesh and the peoples of his cities—Uruk, Ur, Nippur;
the leaping bull-dancers of ancient Crete, the stone portraits

of Athens, the porno-frescoes of Pompeian walls;
Breughel's partying peasants, cod-pieces askew, drunk
and passed out in their fields; the all-consuming Hell
of Hieronymus Bosch— and from there I pass into
my own versions of the sophistications of El Greco,
Rembrandt, Rubens, Durer, da Vinci. My hand wielding
their brushes, my own visions of their subjects, and I am taken
into a long ecstasy, my own mind flowing into theirs—
until there is a sudden change, a surge of pending awareness
and far down the hall I am struck to see my old friend Corozine
painting himself painting his dual portraits of himself
and Monet, himself and Van Gogh, himself and Gaugin,
himself and Gaugin's Tahitian mistress.

I stand behind him absorbed and taken—every move
he makes I make, every move I make he makes—on and on
until I find myself fallen into an elated exhaustion
from which my hand wakes again into the slurp of
the blue-grey present—the so-called "reality" of job and fence,
and I realize the work-day is almost over—

I close the can. Clean the brush.
Section one of the fence is now its assigned color.
I will return tomorrow to continue my studies.

Sacrifices to the God of Poetry, the God of Work Gloves, the
Spirits of these Dead Trees, and the Ego of the Present Poet

Today I'm burning a massive woodpile—Hogan high,
Round, and wide; a lodge for the spirits of these dead trees—
Stumps, roots, broken logs, rotting branches, saplings—
A great tangle of fractured and splintered limbs, grass,
Leaves, loose bark—all of it waiting for the flames—
A conflagration I hope worthy of the poem
That I even now feel rising into being.

To get it started, I've brought along a large bag
Of scrap paper from the last half-year—so full
It's listing with lists, paid bills, news sections,
Abandoned projects, student finals from last semester,
Food boxes, cardboard—all risen from pulp, their origins
Once risen from seed—the common ancestry
Of these trees themselves.

I carry it around the pile, stuffing handfuls as far
As I can reach here and there into every worthy opening.
I've gone around twice this way, when
From near the bottom of the now almost empty bag
I am surprised to pull out a stapled manuscript—
One version of a work sent out to last year's book competitions—
I hadn't been aware that it was in there—and instantly
Stumble into superstition—fearful at first of the meaning
Of this find—the choices it demands.
Then—out of nowhere—I am suddenly overcome
By a profound and deep release—a daring—
A gamble to the gods—quite unlike my usual reactions
To black cats, the numbers 13 or the satanic 666—
Or even 333—its enigmatic half—ever balanced
Between darkness and light—
And to that last inscrutable summation I fling my fate—

And now—in this sudden great burst of careless courage
The kerosene is thrown and spread—and this manuscript
The torch that flares it. And from these flames

I send these poems to you, Apollo, in gratitude
For every poem you've ever helped me build—
May their books rise from this blaze
To someday become my fame—
And may you stay with me in every lamp-lit effort
Through the years to come—Please, I beg,
Make every scribbling count. . . .

And now for you, Atlas, who have served me so well
In this rough work—whose mighty hands
Once balanced the world upon your shoulders,
And whose name has insolently and cynically
Been stolen here—"Atlas/Thermafit/S"—
By small-minded masters of corporate manufacturing
Whose only god is Greed—and placed upon these tight-fitting
And treasured Work Gloves that have served me day by day
Through the last three summers of this rough work,
While your name upon them filled me with delight
And which have just received the last puncture and scorch
To finally make them ready for the fire—
But whose exact replacements I had already
Purchased in affection and foresight—

I now throw these, too, worn, torn, dirty but worthy
And still filled with the sweat of my life—
To these flames in praise and appreciation.
May their flare in this moment illumine
Your dimmed legend from this great distance—
And their new offspring carry on mine
And lend me your strength.

And when that time comes, O Mystery of All,
That my body, too, be given to the fire,
If my name still then be writ in water
Let it rise again someday, I pray, into ink.

An Inquiry into the Contamination of Evidence Concerning the Travels of Marco Polo

There is much to sort out.
Let us begin with the usual simple but suspect proposition:
The Venetian, Marco Polo, made a fabled journey to Cathay.
He became an agent and friend of the Great Khan.
He returned with riches and knowledge.
There were many adventures, many harrowing escapes.

All this happened a long time ago.
The narrative is precise but interpretations
Have trailed off into an entanglement of legends
Snarled by warring schools of theory: The Silk Road Believers,
Those witless slaves to convention. The Lost Taiga Wanderers,
Who claim "The Travels" to have been the forged birch-root
Hallucinations of a demented Russian mystic. Or the so-called
Southern School, Piedmontese monarchists claiming papal descent,
Who'd have Polo meeting Prester John in the southern deserts—
A waste.—The entire landscape, as far as the eye can see.
Too far south. Way off. Nothing there now but mixed gravel
And tank traps. An impossibility. Unless you consider the
All-but-discredited and justly maligned Ibn-Khaloud hypothesis:
The camels galled, sore-footed. Sentries asleep by the fire.
The logic of meaning fragmenting into the perverse
Indiscipline of dream. Everything lost.
Are you paying attention? 5,000 golden ducats per eye-droop
And lions to devour the failures. History an expensive teacher.
No sherbet. No dancing girls. No Ozymandias.
Seven times around the well they were lead
Before the headsman raised his sword.
After That it was too late. Though some might have survived.
The lead horse, given his head, would have led them to water.
Crossing the Empty Quarter would have been costly,
Let alone far off the Mark—(some say a German was with them—
A certain Saxe Gestálte—pronounced phonetically—
A true man of vision who also had a good ear).

Of late objections have been flowing in: "o's", "b's", "j's",
The other seven letters, littering the tidal muck.
Scholars from all disciplines have drawn dissections in the sand.
Visitations reported from as far as Nazca.
Have you ever noticed the apparent
East Asian influences in Peruvian pottery?
Did you know that spaghetti came from China?
It is indisputable that Ural-Altaic bears no kinship to Etruscan.

Does it matter? Some would reply in the obscurantive.
Can condensation forming in a retort be said to be an answer?
If so, can the answer be said to be cloudy?
Am I being retortical in asking?
Are the lights on in Kowloon?

Letter to a Friend following his Suggested Reading of Tomaz Salamun

If I wrote like Tomaz Salamun
you would cast me into the sea.
You would stuff me into the bottle with the *djinn*.
You would unravel every line from the page
and twine them into my noose.
You would send me to Russia to suffer,
never suspecting the depth of my masochism.

If I wrote like Tomaz Salumun
I would be confused.
I would trip on the stairs. I would run into walls.
The irritable stranger in the mirror would try to ignore me.
The flowers in his vase would rise like balloons,
and the world would appear as shards of broken Cyrillic
in which I would encrypt my secret autohagiography.

If I wrote like Tomaz Salamun
and could get away with it, I'd stew the spleens of my critics.
I'd stir the pot and offer them plums.
I'd barge down the Nile and babble in tongues.
I'd drift downstream at six miles an hour
while slattern muses sang in my ears
and you stood on the bank and threw rocks.

"Just a Little Snit, Dear," He Mimics (Silently)
Between Clenched Teeth

"So what's wrong?" I ask her,
trying to sound as innocent and helpful
as my lack of absolute ignorance will allow.
"Oh, nothing," she snaps, "Just a little snit.
I don't want to talk about it. Maybe I'll tell you
after I've thought it over. Or not."

She doesn't have to tell *me* she's in a snit:
I know when I'm being snitsecuted.
Nothing but cold heat from her all day,
and while she's been brusq-ing around
banging her more-together-than-thou
affectations so officiously on the countertops,
I'm the one who's been trying—in my fashion—
to show some restraint. Which hasn't been
made any easier since she passed the prohibition
on passive-aggressive behaviors, which
supposedly leaves me recourse to nothing
but my—of course—innate responsibility,
honesty, and directness.

Isn't that what we (I) agreed to?
To not run regressive spins in the rat cage of compulsion?
To not emit the sullen pings of the submariner of silence?
To not address her, for instance, as I so sorely want to,
in terms of Yes, your Snitjesty, or No, your Snitjesty?
To not slouch around in what she so lovingly calls
my "habitual hangdog skulk", not quite sure
what I've done—or not done—to "deserve"
all this? (I have my suspicions, but even those
are suspect, and anyway, by god, it's too late now.)
Which leaves me right out there, where—
if we follow the logic of contemporary healthfulness—
I must want to be—"off on another self-destructive
spiteful tangent" as she so aptly puts it—
just one more running dog of domesticity
with no tail left to chase but my own.

Lightbulb

I flick the switch and it goes on. Or off.
Or vice-versa, depending on its situation
immediately prior to my flick or an indeterminable
number of other factors, including those which are
internal, such as the relative dependability
of its life-expectancy, or external, such as
the condition of the wiring adjacent to it,
or the reliability of its source of power.
It stares at me from the center of the ceiling,
from street lamps, marquees, headlights,
computer terminals and Christmas trees.
It is a symbol of bourgeois civilization,
which has for the most part already forgotten
its significance. It has been among us,
developing and evolving for well over a century.
The repetition of its singularity gives rise
to the illusion of its ubiquitousness.
It exists in the billions and brings illumination
and comfort to millions. It illumines the plenitude
or emptiness within the allegorical darkness
of the refrigerator. It appears as the
moment of genius in small balloons over
the usually smaller heads of cartoon characters.
It is a cliché of despair dangling naked
from wires in the rooms of paradise denied.
It is the flashbulb of the *paparrazi* of emptiness.
It is the magical demoralized,
the sly metaphor of mystery incarnate:
the body of light embarrassed in a
frosted fishbowl, blushing its radiance
beyond irony and form.

Chartreuse

How

could such

a *purple* word

be green?

Self-Portrait: Aspects of Personality

Larry,
      Curly,
           and Moe

meet

    Dostoevsky.

Without pies . . .

    Too bad.

Third Person First

A glimpse in the mirror
as he leaves the *pissoir* —
"First person singular," he thinks,
then realizes that to say so
puts him back in the third,
the one he likes better on the page—
the self at ego's length
but not separate,
that unembarrassed Siamese twin
connected by pen to persona.—
His own protagonist,
where appraisal is easier
and a pittance more honest
in its balance between ego
and embarrassment: Not objectivity,
but neither is it "abjectivity"
(he knows his weaknesses
all too well).—But if *you*—Yes,
that "you" of the second person,
who are now reading this in my stead,
and thereby connected here by
"thereby", knew him before
you read his work, you
would know that "he" *is* him
and perhaps more free
but no less nor more fiction than "I".

Abandoned Ode to an '82 Toyota

O Miss Silver. O sweetness, O light.
O purring solitude, O jaded rusting beauty.
O faithful thing who thrived on praise.
O my sweet Miss Silver, my back roads beauty,
my tarnished tart, my purring solitude,
my embarrassed trusted pride.
O faithful thing who thrived on praise;
who loved your dashboard patted,
your wheel caressed,
your little love-horn teased—
I, who for nine of your seventeen years,
was the flesh that filled your shell,
I, who was your essence, your soul, your spark—
the principle which enlivened you,
have betrayed you this day for $300,
signed the documents, taken the money,
become your shameless guiltless Judas.

I had not known that parting would be so joyous.
I, who had long feared a worse outcome to this day,
had never seen you before as I did
when you stood before me this morning—
your doors and trunk gaping open,
suddenly an obscenity, an empty hulk
of mockery, void of life ,
vitality, meaning—I suddenly saw you
as sloughed off skin, an empty tortoise,
a paradigm of depression, a nothingness
of metal, a delusion, a trick I had
played on myself—and in this soulless
scornful freedom, I turn away from you now

to my new love, Ms. Mazda, this black beauty
half your age, this present to my poverty
into whom I enter gently now as though
she were a trusting, welcoming, virgin.

"Ampersand,"

          I scrawl, & image wells through word
from the brilliant darkness. Leaps the wildness
of synapse between the text of the body
& the text of the mind; between the I & the world
        &
being & meaning & the ceaseless choices in all.
Sees its symbol & seizes its shape—
Squats on the page like that Fat Goddess of fertility
offering up her bowl of abundance—that
ebulliently-buttocked mother of the Western soul
found in middens from the Dordogne to Palestine
        &
still with us in psyche & soma,
our selves & collective self, our mathematics
& our poetics, our multiplicities,
our burgeoning experiences, our awareness
of the ever-expanding universe,
our compulsion to connect
        &
find purpose, the incessant tumescence
& release of desire, the infinitely unbounded
bounty & tragedy of existence,
the endless & triumphant
always new & next fullness
& "and" of it all, & so on, &tc. . . .

Ellipsis . . .

```
                              *   *
                               *
                               *
                           Two-
                          minded
                       serpent of si-
                          lence . . .
                           hiss-
                            ing
                          through
                      the high grass
                       of meaning . . .
                 spine of cen-
               sure and subtlety
              struggling against
            itself . . . division de-
             veloped into duality
                . . . the little stars of its aster-
                   isk vertebrae erasing the l*tt*rs
                       but leaving the words to laugh
                          at the censor; the sly
                         periods of its ribs . . .
                     sliding into insinuat-
                   ions of understand-
                  ing . . . the contract-
                  ions of knowing;
               a wink, a nod to
              the unspoken
              . . . trailing off
             into the shu-
              sh of omis-
                 sion . . . with . . .
                    . . . and/or
                      without
                         . . . its  s  i  n  s . . . .
```

V. The Music He Hears is Witness

My Thoughts Rise from the Earth Like Branches, Like Antlers ...

A warm rain in January.
The dying snow gives up its substance to the Shades;
A thickening fog obscures the world.
The day drifts on slowly into a gray wilderness.
These woods have invited me into their latitudes of silence:
The rest is a waiting, a watch, a willingness—
A wealth of images suddenly welling—

My thoughts rise from the earth like branches, like antlers;
Wet, dark, fecund, generative. Springing from the ground,
Flowing out, each following each,
Multiplying into vast forests, nimble herds;
Great migrations advancing, retreating,
Appearing and disappearing,
Falling back into the mists
Like ages, like ruins, like tribes.

Crow Morning

A sudden alarm
on a long walk in the snow.

Incredible, how
for just one moment,
with all time
alive around it,
three crows rise
from a pine top
to fill
this blue morning
with all hope,
all memory,
all meaning.

March 1ˢᵗ, False Spring

Sun abounding in snow -
Listen: The world is melting. -
Laughter in water
   murmuring deceptions
      through teeth of rotting ice;
tinkling promises whispered
in the metamorphosis
   of forms,
the conversion of energy,
the choiceless acquiescence of matter
in the integrity of physics.

Twenty days to the equinox:
the latitude tilts toward hope.
All around, the air rises thick with thaw,
ripe with agitation and indolence;
the smell of earth and light,
of memory and yearning.

The warm spring welling,
it's budding beauty
blind to the betrayal
lurking in the frozen
sod below.

The Gift

It was April, the night of my birthday that year
and I'd wandered out toward the pond just to be there.
A light snow earlier had fallen over the older,
packed layers, and the moon had come out full and bright
to fill that white dusting on the pine boughs
with a ghostly brilliance, a radiant halo glow.
I'd walked down the road and paused by the last field
before the woods when I first heard it—as though
it had waited for that exact moment of my attention—
A long, slow, deep howl rising up into the night—
a sound I'd wanted all of my life to hear, but—
raised as I'd been on all those old rumors of the wolf's return—
never thought that I would—

I stood there fixed, alert—the night itself alive around me—
Then it came again—a long, deep, beautiful howl
reaching out into that frozen stillness.
I could tell where it was—down in the low, wet woods
below the dam, about a half-mile away—
Closer this time, coming upstream, following the brook.
I started walking again, almost running, toward the dam,
hoping to see it, and as I went I heard it twice more,
closer each time. I got to the bridge over the little neck of water
flowing from the pond to the dam and stuck there, stock-still,
staring down into the woods and that long silence,

and nothing happened. Gradually the intensity faded.
I gave up and turned away, back toward the pond,
and there it was—out on the ice, barely a hundred feet away.
Still, silent, standing sideways, ears cocked, grey fur glowing
in full moonlight, watching me. We both held there
for a long, long moment, taking each other in.
I thanked him. I thanked him from all of my years, until at last
he trotted slowly, calmly, off the ice into the brush,
disappearing into the darkness beneath those luminous pines,
into the mythos of that moment—its radiance still within me,
deep and alive every time I open it again.

Waiting for Persephone

It is March. Late March. The drag end of March,
scraping like an anchor across the bottoms of his brain-pan.
The slowest season in the slow-turning calendar of his years.
The persistence of rotting snow, the raw mockery
of a gray sun, of hard winds driven from a bitter sky.
Every year he does what he promises himself he won't do:
Suffers the last meanness of winter like an adolescent
craving the still-distant delights of first love.
Leans into Spring with the full weight of his heart.
Strains to lever life upward from the frozen mud,
the long tilt of the planet. Breathes on the tinder
of longing like the coals in his stove.
Listens for the gutter of time in every thawing rivulet.
Watches for the signs: The droop of catkins
forming in the aspens, the red haze
gathering in the maples,
a deepening blush in the birch-tops.
He wants to sleep, to hoard the changes
like fluids in his body.
To dream past the distance of April,
the crowns of skunk cabbage
rising from brown litters,
the chorused curl of fiddleheads,
the thick throw of bluets at the meadow's edge—
To wake at last to the green trumpets of fullness,
their lush treasures overflowing an emerald world.

Specks in the Ointment

In the pre-dawn gloom of my waking
A fly is attempting to speak to me.
An early fly, a most unseasonable fly.
A pink, distinctly human tongue struggles
against the mangling bites of furious mandibles.
It is trying to tell me something of our common nature,
a relationship which I do not want and did not ask for.
Its buzzing irritates me almost beyond endurance,
yet the false compassion of courtesy bids me
to listen for speech I suspect but cannot hear.

In the thousand reflections of each eye
I recognize the sufferings of a fellow being.
In each facet quivers a different image --
a spider, the ceiling, my own distorted features,
the lamp, the dresser, all the kaleidoscopic
commonplaces of our mutual situation.

I strain my own eyes toward him, seeking larger meanings.
I want to experience the profundity of this moment.
I want irrefutable evidence of spiritual connection,
a distinct sign in each refraction of his vision:
a planet warm and turning, for instance,
or a tiny moon in orbit, frowning, and beyond the moon
galaxies whirling pinwheels of delight.
But I see only the ranks of my own mirrored features
staring back in their agonized legions.

So much I could tell him. So much hope to be given:
In these latitudes the manure of south-facing pastures is far richer
than the sun-deprived patties of the northern slopes.
A dead fox lies in the alders behind our neighbor's barn.
It is March. The mud time is coming.
New seed will soon take, and our fortunes lie fallow.
Under the frozen sod lie regions of great turmoil
and transformation.

June Evening

The hills are dark,
the nearer woods, darkening,
the last blue of day a deep luminescence
failing in the West.
Twilight edges down and outward
stealthily, with the deer,
deepening into the borders
of the meadows, slowly, faithfully,
enveloping all things
in its essence; darkness
filling the ditches, overflowing
and spreading; rising through
the high, thick, sweet smelling grass,
upward into a dusk filled
with the warm, deep pungency
of absent cattle.

Two whip-poor-wills call
from the cover of their thickets.
A fox barks once
from the far edge of the field.
A chorus of frogs gathers and rises
from the trough-pond, as though
in ecstasy to a low, sickle moon,
to metamorphosis,
and the first stars.

A mile away a small plane strobes
across the darkness, pulsing red and green,
droning its way back
into the familiarity of my childhood.
And look!—the first fireflies!
In fifty years, I've already
lived a long life—
Another good day today,
and now all this rapture
rising into night!

Crickets, Frogs, Fireflies, Owls, and Cosmos

Tonight, out here on the edge of this meadow I call my Star Field,
where I come many nights to follow the constellations
through their seasons, I am greeted not by the usual chorus
of frogs—but on this night a full orchestra—many more frogs
than I'd ever heard here before—all of them accompanied
loudly and fully by the trilling of an exultant chorale of crickets—
a resonant, strong, symphony—an elation to my ears—all conducted
by two owls—one inside the edge of the woods to the north, the
other in the nearer woods to the south—all of this crowned by a
glimmering cosmos of fireflies—many more of them, too, than
I'd thought I'd see—their slow iridescences wavering, hovering,
gliding, but rising, spreading, filling their elevation as though
in praise of all below and all the cosmic beauty in the sky above—
their glory to it accentuated by the sudden flash of two meteorites—
one following immediately behind the other, their alarm
drawing my eye upward beyond their passage to bring me back
into the mission of my delight—to circle again through the
                                                    illumined
mysteries in the towering infinity above—first to the brightest,
Jupiter, up under the long magnificence of Leo, then east to Spica,
just above Scorpio with Antares, its pulsing yellow heart—
and above all that Great Red Mars, brighter now than it's been
in years. I swing my gaze far back to the west beyond Leo to
                                                    Gemini,
then circle northward past Perseus to Cassiopeia the Queen,
and east again beyond her to the wide, long, Summer Triangle—
Deneb in Cygnus, Vega in Lyra, Altair in Aquila—and there,
high above all, Polaris and its Bears and between them the long
reptilian curl of Draco the Dragon, its diamond head about to strike
at Hercules, while all the while here, below, in the little galaxy
of this meadow the concert continues, an exhilaration flaring
in all the space around and within it and I am held here filled
with its energy, my body rocking, brimming with it, my feet
pacing in place as I utter little prayers of thanks to every star,
every planet, every constellation, every cricket in their chorale,
every frog in their concert, every hooting of the owls, every firefly
become starfly, every deep wonder of this night.

Horse Tale

On that summer afternoon when he was six years old
and they told him that those high many-plumed grasses
out on the frontier between the yard and the woods
were called "horsetail" he galloped out into the herd—
played and played, rode and rode—raced, bucked
into stampede, round-up, rustlers, raids; charged the fort,
outrode the posse of supper time until they reined him in,
made him sit at the table, mind his manners,

then eased up after he'd eaten, let him charge back out—
A one-kid cavalry through early evening, twilight
drawing down its shades on the day's adventures
until they pulled him back in again
with their gentle coaxing lasso of love
and at last he dismounted the day, let them put him to bed,
where he nodded off to the whinny of grasses
whispered by the breezes outside his open window.

The All-ness of It Everywhere

Not God he calls it, but the Mystery of Existence—
of Being. Something he can see whenever
he opens his eyes and looks with his mind.
The Oneness of it. The all-ness of it everywhere.
His being just one cell in the body of Cosmos,
its flawed mirror the billions of cells in his own,
the universe of atoms in each blending him into infinity.
   His delight in the profundity of not-knowing.
No rules save nature groping its way through time.
No Holy Writ. No Clergy. No Chosen—
   But note how he honors it with capitals,
the language in which he frames it.
That one good grace left over from Sunday school.
   Then there's the fact that he talks to it. Often.
Especially up here by this narrow bend of river
he keeps returning to. Not expecting an answer.
Nor a listener. Except himself. His part simply
to take in what he says, then let it abide.
   Up here just now he's happy. In his place.
Steep woods on one bank, flat field on the other.
Steps up to that open space over the water;
thanks the day for filling him with its life—

An alarmed beaver startles him!—
slaps its tail and dives!—

. . . The day smiling back at the man . . .

Stone Over Water

Down at the landing this morning
there's no horizon, only fog, a gray silence
swirling slowly, listening to itself. He sees a mast
moored in the mist, its reflection swimming
like a snake across the near-calm water.
He closes his eyes and it still crosses toward him.
Opens them again and everything is lost
in shifting veils. His mind skips across memory
like a stone over water. The curl of trails
when he was a boy growing up in the mountains.
Or writhing in the torments of first love
through the long nights of Darmstädt.
Or Helga on Crete a decade later,
camped on the rainy beach.
Her newness to him; the strength of her body.
The strange strong length of her neck
as she moved under him. The sounds that she made,
far off and near, like that buoy he hears now,
a low bell, irregular and languorous,
rolling slowly on an unseen tide.

Different Waters Flowing

The third person: He realizes again
how he likes to think of himself this way,
knowing it's a ruse. Closing the I and opening the eye.
The historical perspective allows a compassion for faults
he knows he wouldn't otherwise forgive.
Makes room for mistakes, revises understanding
along the paths through the errors of his ways,
the losses in time better lost. Tonight
he remembers Karen, then decides not to. It's been
too long to bother. Listens to the rain, the frogs in the pond.
Watches himself as he watches himself equivocate.
Thinks instead of the slow winding of a sandy-bottomed river
then remembers her again, swimming in the clear
sandy flow of another. Remembers first her nakedness;
the swirling lure of her sex in the water.
Remembers her name: *the dark one.*
The flawless place between her legs.
The pain of memory accentuated in the mystery of her body.
Years of other women since he'd thought of her this way.
Tonight he leaves himself out. Swims between her thighs
with his mind only. His awareness not a longing but water,
a mink watching under the bank, a meditation of trout,
the silken current that tastes her form,
a rippling clarity coursing through a weir of yearning.

"*Midnight*", *You Said*

"Midnight",
you said,
from above me;
your body
ascendant
in a field
of stars.

Your breasts
glowed like worlds
in the luminous
     darkness,
and a red moon rode
through the depths
of your belly
over a longing
that drew me
into your ocean
like the tide.

Sweet Weight

Once, long ago, on a
train platform in Thessalonika,
I suddenly remembered,
too late,
the sweet weight
of your breast
in my palm.

Tonight, years later,
I remember remembering—
Once again, suddenly;
once again,
too late;
once again,
sweetly.

Still so Many

He thinks of a man thinking of himself.
Wonders again what it would be like
to be a stranger in the mirror.
Whether or not he could imagine his life
honored with other sufferings.
He smiles when he thinks of his luck.
How his being is always re-filling,
buoying him on through its mysteries,
with still so many yet to come.
He wonders at his wonderings and listens
to the crickets. The way their song from
his history sings through the sweet distances
of the wilderness within....

An August night; *the Golden Month*,
he likes to call it. High summer, the season
changing season. The last fireflies already gone,
flaring out like dying Gauls. He has an old wish,
a sentimentality he allows himself:
When the time comes to die, he wants
to die in summer. Sitting alone
in an old meadow, facing the mountains.
The skeletal trees, snow and bitter earth of winter
waiting for him still months in the future,
waiting for a shadow that never comes.
One last good gift to his life: to drift away
with the crickets, his spirit passing
without notice into a silence haunted by owls.

Samsara in Richmond, Maine

From the Russian Church
after a long hot ride
through a humid August afternoon,
I hear the singing of the priest,
clear and liquid,
like the babble of a summer brook,
trickling
down the liturgy
of the Resurrection.

Later,
down by the river,
under the broad cool leaves
of this agnostic evening,
anchored boats nod slowly
in a current
indifferent to atonement,
oblivious of salvation,
murmuring
only
of eternal
return.

Equinox In A Later Autumn

How the seasons flow now into confluence
in these new days, this new history
gathering in the blood,
these lives of a lifetime
flowing into one.
Like a memory from Gaul,
like some old Roman flourishing in his exile,
I rejoice in the perspective of this solitary place,
in this clean air fragrant with warmth,
sweet with chill;
this clear cold dark stream
and the forest out for miles around me,
these vast woodlands now returned,
green leaves scorched to rust in high September,
where farms had once been cleared from wilderness.

So, too, these onward changes in the lands within.
An ancient sadness from my teething years
falling away,
falling away behind me.
All the old dreads now diminished,
drowning in the clarity of their passage.
This slow learning brightening in the veins;
this slow turning
leeching the bitterness
from the bone.

The Music He Hears is Witness,

Life vibrating through stillness,
following him wherever he goes.
The steam locomotives of his childhood
wailing through the moonless distances
of the long winter nights of West Virginia.
The dark alien hills echoing them
through his longing for a far-off summer morning
and the sharp song of blue jays in the pitch pines
of his Adirondack mountain home.

The light changing through fifty years,
only recently lifting its weight.
But the sounds carrying through.
His mother calling his name.
Later other women saying it differently.
One sound enters another and changes it,
the drift of his life in their resonance:

The nightly coyotes on Olsen's farm.
The wolf that winter at Runaround Pond.
The peepers in spring, cicadas in August;
Now in October the circle of owls in hemlock and oak.
The silence toward dawn and the crows waking to light.
The breeze rising and the air humming,
listening for itself and answering.

VI. Mantras From the Deep World

Ancestry
(Bracketed and italicized refrains to be sung as Gregorian chants)

My life is mind, is matter,
is dry bone and wet flesh,
labor of love and dance of death,
mandrake root in Eden's sod—
   [sprung from the seed of a hanged god—
   glorious turnip; corn off the old cob, I am]—
ash of Adam and horn of Pan.

My earth is lime, is loam,
is petrified bone in suffering stone,
dung of hoof and blood of man,
grass of veldt and flow of sand.

My voice rises from the sleep of stone,
from the fossilized speech of a dead jawbone
loosed by flood from millennial clay,
from the Rift of time to the light of day,

spitting out teeth and the muffling earth,
giving sound to thought
in the slowly found tongue,
born to its ear and the voices beyond,
to glottal stops and the ¡click! of ¡*K'ung!*

Speaking in kind to the gurgle of brooks,
to the singing stones and the whispering vines,
to the murmuring streams of bicameral mind;
to the hooting of owls and the howling of wolves,
and the speech of gods and the glory of dawn.

My song rises through the reed of bone,
through the vibrant organs of my fleshly home.
Song of Solomon, Epic of Ur,
an upright stance in the stretched femur.
Dance of David in an opera grand,
all the vices of a growing brain pan.

My seed formed in the great Dream Time,
in the dust of stars from the last Big Bang
through the swirl of vapors to the first-formed slime.—
methane, formeldahyde, ammonia gases,
complex carbons, protocells—
Paradise rose from its seasons in hells.

Neuron, synapse, primitive tissues,
that's how cosmos commenced our issue.—
        [Spine of serpent, hypocampus,
        limbic system, that's our context,
        delusions to contrary in the neocortex.]

Mind rising up from the seed of being,
and the rising of dream from the soil of mind,
and the longing of flesh for its kindred kind,
and the lust for power and the need to know.

Sired by astrologers, foaled by stars:
Venus, Andromeda, Astarte, Mars;
priest and priestess, temple prostitute—
        [begotten in the bellies of the holy whores of Babylon—
        Zygote of the Ziggurat, chip off the old icon,
        I am.]—

Womb of Europa, bull of Zeus,
sons of Han, Dukes of Ch'ou,
bone of Roman, stones of Gaul,
electron, proton, Shiva's dance;
sperm meets egg and the bastard is Chance.

My death shadows in the rippling noon,
in the next breath drawn in my fear of doom,
in the dead light cast by the corpse of moon,
in the dance of atoms in their deathless trance,
one to another in a waltz sublime
in the endless nuance of immortal time.

Atom from atom, thus I'll pass
from bone to stone, to earth, to tree,
to blood, to soil, to flower, to bee,
to whatever form I'm taken
and someday yet may the flesh reawaken.

Dispose of the body through fire or worm,
the result is still eternal return;
not soul, nor thought, nor human, may be,
but matter is matter through rot or burn
and all matter's one in the same mystery.

The Ur-Word

Before the beginning there was No Thing; not time, nor light,
    nor space— A formlessness without measure; neither
    great nor small, finite nor infinite, and from that no-thing
    formed one atom, the egg of existence, and
    within that atom curled the Ur-Word; the primal noun,
    the quantum verb of causation, the metaphor of
    metaphors, the lingua spiritus of all things yet to
    become; the mind of Cosmos dreaming in the
    promised joy of its substance.

And then there was Light; the waiting birth of Ur-energy,
    conceiving itself in particle and wave; the birth of
    Being from Nothingness itself; a slow-burgeoning fruit
    budding from the chrysalis of Idea, swelling, bursting
    into flower, into a clarity from which was created
    the possibility of all things within it; the Ur-word first
    shifting and chirping and chipping at its shell.

Millennia fled before memory, eons passed without witness.
    Thus did the Ur-word become itself waiting itself:
    Ur is patience filling with passion.

The patience of Ur is tireless; the tirelessness of Ur fills all
    potential, broods and waits in all things still yet to become.
Ur is the essence of the living essential; essence waiting to
    become urge. When perceived in fear, Ur spreads
    destruction; is destructiveness itself.
    When perceived in light, Ur manifests in nobility of spirit,
    in creation, in courage.
Ur is cunning, the phantom precursor of cleverness. Ur holds shy
    of consciousness, wishing to remain in the primordial.
Ur slurs in the drunk, purrs in the lover, dreams in the sleeping soul.
Ur blooms quietly in desolation, in emptiness. Ur sleeps in ruins,
    dreams in abandoned places.
Ur wanders in the desert wind, vitalizes the wilderness with its
    thought, with the vast and boundless dancing of Mind.

Ur flares in the magmatic flame of the deep earth, manifests in the
fiery rivulet of molten gold seeking its way upward toward
light, even as it cools into a vein of rich and amnesiac ore.
It was this latent memory of Ur-gold which the mind of the
alchemist sought, unaware of its origins or the true nature
of his quest.

Ur is born into the quivering cell; into life, multiplicity, growth,
purpose, senescence and death. Returning to the soil,
Ur hardens in the sediment, metamorphoses life into stone,
stone into life, moment into eon. Ur ticks in the clock,
biding its time.
Ur denies its existence; disguises itself as delusion, cloaks
itself as a lie: Ur conceals itself as the conceit of the poet,
the furtive inkling of a too-fertile mind; a febrile answer
to the curse of the unanswerable question.

Ur was there in the first gifts of consciousness, risen into the gods of
rivers, of beasts, of earth and grain and the knowledge of their
use, in spirits of place and powers of purpose. Ur entered the
dreams of Gilgamesh and Enkidu, singing their lives in blood
and in being, blessing their city with the pre-conscious
memory of its name.
Ur raised the first towns, dreaming geometry and structure, filling
minds with the need to build and to order, to concentrate
and refine, to perfect and define.
Ur rose from the dark earth of excavation into the light
of scholarship, where it was betrayed by intellect,
whored by ambition.
The Ur of the ancients is not the Ur of the philologist, the arche-
ologist, the historian. Ur is the hope of the past,
the memory of the future.

Ur breathes its Word by its nature, gurgles in the voice of the
infant. Ur is the impulse of tale, of saga and epic. Ur
strikes the spark from the brimstone of literature.
Thus is Ur also the urge of irony, of satire.

Ur delights in the jealous arrogance of the poet, who sings Ur's
    praises as though Ur was for poets alone. Ur gets the joke,
    and it isn't on Ur.

Ur finds its way, fulfilling the way of all things sentient and of all
    things non-sentient, organic and non-organic, all things
    born of becoming.
Ur rises in the forces lifting from the warm earth, drifts in the
    clouds, falls again earthward with the healing rain,
    the destroying storm; the inexorable passage
    of flood and fertility.
Ur slumbers in the slow-moving glaciers, the crush of pack-ice,
    the millennial depth of polar snows; smiling in its dream,
    stirring in its sleep.

Ur flows from the springs, drifts in the deep lakes; animates
    the trout and the bullhead, the muskrat
    and the otter.
Ur nurtures the oceans, curls through their currents,
    surges the depths of the deep-welling sea.
Ur breathes through the gills of the cruising shark, whispers
    seductively in the silver trail of the whale's wake.

Ur turns slowly in the orbit of the night-riding moon, waxing
    and waning, pulling the tides of ocean and mind
    through the parallax ellipses of unending time.
Ur pulses in the quasar, throbs in the heart. Ur is the blood of light,
    the light welling in the pulsing blood
Ur orders disorder, causes the antagonism of opposites,
    the balance of oppositions.
Ur suffers in the shadowed soul, heals in the balming light,
    creates pain and surcease from pain; fills the heart
    with terror and tenacity, with horror and calm,
    all for the way of its purpose,
    all for the flow of becoming.

Ur murmurs through the course of my blood, whispers these lines
into being; fills my mind with their sound.
Ur whispers, Ur gurgles, Ur murmurs, Ur lurks, Ur urges,
Ur pulses, Ur breathes; Ur nurtures all things
through their being, fills all things with its song.

A Mantra from The Deep World

—What thou lovest well remains,
What thou lovest well is thy true heritage
What thou lovest well shall not be reft from thee....

—Ezra Pound, *Pisan Cantos*, LXXXI

At the center of my being pivots an orrery of dimensionless
    galaxies - changing, ever-shifting, flowing endlessly
    through the flux and spiral of the always becoming.
My mind is one among billions, an atom of the world's mind,
    and within that atom, I am a world within the world;
    an atlas of mind surveying itself;
    this world opening to all worlds,
    the great longing of being for itself.
My thoughts abandon form to fluidity and flow into one another.
    Everything I know I am still learning.
    Everything I have forgotten
    is still within me, always changing,
    always in motion, always waiting.

       *   *   *

Within me opens a geography of continents and islands,
    of bright seas and cold oceans.
Here are the depths of heaven and the fathomless deep:
    My tides sweep my estuaries, my banks, my rivers.
    My currents curl deep through the songs of my tropics,
    winding their life through straits and archipelagos
    of distance and mystery.
The seas around me are beautiful and wondrous,
    are dreadful and deep.
I bask and dream in the warmth of my shallows.
I feel a cold fear and a darkness in
    the fathomless plumb of my depths—
    the depths where no life or unknown life lies:
    beyond my banks, beyond my shelves—

the cold depths below even unconsciousness;
    the waiting depths of all darkness,
And of this serpent coiling within me, I seek to shed my fear
    as it sheds its skin,
    to become the sensory coil of life opening to all mystery.

        *   *   *

This Deep World flows through me in ebb and in flow
    and is seen and remembered, realized and forgotten,
    passing on to the next remembrance.
In the fields of night I am a questioner of Time,
    an archeologist of the living stars.
I dream the thin air brilliant among the high peaks of my mountains,
    range after range marching across the horizon.
I have been a wind in the deserts, a small, dark funnel of being
    unto itself, rising and falling, whirling here and there,
    passing slowly on its journey as though musing,
    a sentient breeze.

        *   *   *

I have been the bending trees, the boughs lifting and falling
    through the storms of my forests.
I have been the mute stones watching, the silence waiting
    on the sides of the mountains.
In the mornings I slip warily through the forests and hills.
In the afternoons I stand naked on the sands of these
    meandering rivers.
In the forests and the seasons I read the changes of growth
    and decline, and chart them in my imagination.
In my essence I am a messenger between worlds,
    between plant and animal,
    between the generations before and the generations after.
    I am the elements of the message itself, encoded in plasma,
    sealed in this animal flesh.

My bone is limestone, my marrow the carved and silted caverns
    of earth's history.
I feel the lairs in my forests, the dens in my great hollows.
    In this near-darkness I perceive dimly the breathing of fur,
    the tense and silent unlidding of eye,
    the slow stirring of tooth and claw.
I hold within me prairie, veldt, tundra, savannah; great plains
    still hardly known to me from equator to arctic.
    Vast geographies of my interior are still trackless
    from my step.
My jungles are thick, greener than green, secretive—
    festooned with delusions; fecund with life, with fur and claw,
    feather, swarm, and scale.

*   *   *

This deep world opens to the entirety of all being;
    to wonder, to intellect,
    to all senses, to imagination, intuition.
    I feel myself contemporary
    with all time, all mind, all nature that my species has known.
    This date is not my only dimension; this place
    is not my only province.
My mind is an anthropology of psyches, a history of being.
    I dream the tribes in my hills, the canoes drifting my rivers,
    the nomads among my deserts and plains,
    my lost cities dreaming life.
The time that I breathe in is this time and all time.
    I have breathed the air of Nineveh and Ur.
I understand the quest of Gilgamesh, the guilt of Raskolnikov,
    the innocence of Myshkin, the folly of Quixote.
Something within me has always understood this.
    This Deep World has been mine
    since before my beginning.
The flux of all history drifts down my blood. Within me flows
    the river of change, the dance of Shiva in the void of Eternity.

Within me are male and female, darkness and light,
    Eros and Thanatos, the passive and the demanding,
    giver and receiver,
    truth and lie, lover and hater,
    life and death.
My character flows in streams above and below the surface;
    expands, contracts, rises, falls, changes and is never still.
My weaknesses are the flaws of my strengths;
    my strengths the surrender of my weaknesses.
Within myself I hold all the ages of my own mortality,
    yet I am ageless, universal.
    Within me are the child, the youth, the ancient—
    I am all of these selves and all of their manifestations
    at any moment.

            *   *   *

I am a lover of humanity, but distant and wary of it.
    Yet all that I love and all that I am wary of,
    I hold within me.
In the course of my life no thought, no desire, no hidden motive,
    no secret has been beyond me.
Within me are the Tarot of the human;
    the oppositions of the humanly possible:
    the assassin and the angel, the fanatic and the sage.
    the hangman and the hero, the accused and the judge.
My heart is at once noble and depraved.
I am endless hope and bottomless despair.
I am the sword in the Lake,
    the Grail of my own existence.

            *   *   *

I am a man who is a man like the fox.
    When you have seen me, you have seen me
    walking only the edges of your fields.
    We have rarely met. I prefer the company of trees,
    the intelligence of the ancient wise,
    the freedom of the vision behind my own eyes.
I spend more time in the forest than I do with my fellows.
I have been a fool to fools, as they are to me.
    My vigil is kept in separateness;
    within my darkness snarl the dogs
    of arrogance and rejection.
I have walked long nights in the pain of my difference,
    the suffering of my sameness.
Yet I abide in my flux, in my struggle with acceptance
    of the unacceptable, in my faith in the infinitude
    of mysteries of which my flux, my change, is part.

            *   *   *

I am a vessel filled with light, a vessel filled with darkness.
I am a vessel filled with time and memory
    and foreknowledge hidden from myself.
I open to my darkness. I open to my light.
    I open to the meaningfulness
    that flows ever through me,
    to the wisdom of all Being,
    the wisdom beyond knowledge.
I dance in my darkness. I dance in my light.
    I dance in the shadows of flickering night.
I am the hunter and I am the prey.
    I am the arrow which knives through my heart.
I am the magician and I am his being.
    I am the antlers rising through mist
    toward the morning.
I feel the cavern opening toward light.

I am an alchemist of the certain knowledge of Unity.
I feel the Earth alive with energies of Cosmos.
I feel the winds blowing through the purifications
    of a thousand autumns.
I see the winds gouging and tearing, hurling and reeling,
    calming and keeling, balming and healing.
I feel the flow of the waters through endless millennia.
I feel myself become one with the surge of whispering rivers,
    with the fountains rising in a hundred ancient cities.
I am the air breathing itself over the mountain vastnesses
    of the great North.
    I am the gentle lift under the wings of the desert kite.
    I am in the living breath of an infinity of souls
    scattered through countless unknown towns.
I breathe and open to the violet unseen light of origin.
I open to the light emanating from within me—
I breathe and energy passes through me.
I breathe and light rises within me.
I breathe and my body draws earth into itself.
I breathe and within myself I feel the rise
    of clay, soil, rock, mulch, vegetation.
I breathe and in the depth of my slow and steady pulse
    I see the migrations of peoples, the rise of civilizations,
    the surge and flow of hordes,
    the decline of conquering armies. . . .

       *   *   *

I breathe in my silence in the forest
    and hear the forest gathering around me.
    I hear the gathering sounds of dawn, of morning, of noon.
    I hear the sounds of afternoon,
    the gathering sounds of evening, of dusk.

I wait in the forest and listen.
I listen in the forest.
I listen in the forest.
I listen in the forest.

I listen.

VII. Understory

Understory

The old man had always been a mystery,
living out there on that abandoned logging road
in those miles of woods between the Parsonsfields.
Months would go by without anyone seeing him;
no one even noticed when he first went missing.
Gone for all of seven seasons before a hunter found him—
not in those open pine woods where they'd sometimes
seen him ranging, but tangled in brush beneath the understory
less than a hundred yards behind his shack.
Stripped down to rags on a skeleton, bedded
in spears of burdock; ribs twined with creeper;
his skull filled now with the strangeness of other life,
the sun tracking its daily course of shadow and light
along the brow of the caves where his eyes had been.

No one knew of anyone to claim him.
When they went in to clean out his place,
not expecting much—a rotting cot,
a very old sleeping bag, a few utensils, one tin cup—
it was the notebooks that surprised them:
Piles upon piles of old notebooks, all of them full—
"Crawling with words," someone said. A library of wildness—

Journal entries that seemed written by the forest itself;
the woods he lived in become the woods living in him.
Passages of a feral intelligence hedging off into its hinterlands—
Stories of stones, autobiographies of trees—a runic hand-scrawl
scratching itself into granite, sand, leaf, bough, fin, fur,
feather, claw; the commonality of blood and bone and branch—
Histories of a self gone Other.

After the Cremation

Do this for me:
Honor why I chose the fire
Against the other; preferring
The darkness of night with its stars
To the darkness of the grave;
The free flight of essence in its instant
To the slow moldering of putrefaction.

Take me to the mountain, and
For one last moment remember me as I was,
Then fling me outward—(not "back,"
For there is no return, only change; the
Continuous transformation of origin)—
Outward into every-ness:
Ashes to air, atoms to elements,
To join the flight of forms
Already freed by the fire
Carried by wind and light
Particle and wave.

Let my carbon become fuzz of sumac,
Leaf of oak, commonality of flesh,
Vein of coal and flame of forest;
My iron enter into earth and platelet of blood;
My hydrogen and oxygen into water and air;
My bone into calcium; my calcium into
The limestone barrow.

Send me quickly, that I may
Once again freely enter into the many
Which form the mystery of the All.

Acknowledgments

Chapbook:
Moon Pie Press: *The Ur-Word,* October, 2008: 27 poems

Literary Magazines:
New Millennium Writings, 2017. (Forthcoming) "Waiting for
Persephone" (Honorable Mention), also appeared in *The Ur-Word.*

New Millennium Writings, 2016. Two poems, "Under the Sign of
Kronos" (Honorable Mention, Short-listed for Winner), "Specks in
the Ointment"also in *Stolen Island Review,* Sping, 2003, (Honor-
able Mention). Both also appear in *The Ur-Word.*

New Millennium Writings, 2015. Two poems, "Bittersweet" (Honor-
able Mention), "To the Bronze lady of Xanthos Found in the Deep,
This Fragment, Too Late, from My Loss" (Honorable Mention).

New Millennium Writings, 2013. One poem, "Sanding Blue Doors"
(Honorable Mention, Short-listed for Winner), also appeared in
Stolen Island Review, Spring, 2003. "Understory" (awarded shared
First Prize, $500) also appeared in *The Portland Sunday Telegram,*
June 16, 2013. Both poems also in *The Ur-Word.*

New Millennium Writings, 2012. Two poems: "Ancestry," (Honor-
able Mention),"Consciousness" (Honorable Mention). Also in *The
Ur-Word.*

New Millennium Writings, 2011. Two poems: "Interlinear" (First
Prize, $1,000), "Mystery Incarnate" (Honorable Mention). Both in
The Ur-Word.

Poetry Miscellany, Winter, 2002: "An Inquiry Into the Contamina-
tion of Evidence Concerning the Travels of Marco Polo," also in *The
Ur-Word.*

Animus, #7 Winter/Spring 2002, and *The Ur-Word.* One poem:
"Ice Night."

Puckerbrush Review, Summer/Fall, 2001, and *The Ur-Word*. One poem: "Crow Morning."

The Contemporary Review, July, 2001, and *The Ur-Word*. One poem: "Letter to Richard Jackson Following His Suggested Reading of Tomaz Salamun."

Cafe Review, Vol. 10, Fall, 1999, and *The Ur-Word*. Two poems: "To Old Yuan Chi, a Fond Reply," and "Philosophy and Ostracism, Athens, 1975."

So What? 1997. One poem, "Midnight, You Said."

Cafe Review, Vol. 3, No. 7/8, 1993. 6-page poem, re-titled: "Mantra From The Deep World."

Cafe Review, Vol. 2, No. 1, 1991. Three poems: "Sweet Weight," "Chartreuse," "Notes from the Holocene."

Café Review, Vol. 1, No. 9, 1990. Three poems: "Spoor," "Under the Sign of Kronos," "My Thoughts Rise From the Earth like Branches, Like Antlers."

Other poems from *The Ur-Word* also included here: "Found Poet," "Still So Many," "Exile," "Stray," "After the Cremation," and "Ampersand," and "Spoor."

I wish to thank all of the journals listed above for their publication of my poems. I especially wish to thank Don Williams, founder and editor emeritus of ***New Millennium Writings***, and his daughter, Alexis Williams Carr, its present editor, for their appreciation—and, indeed—honoring—of my work, and encouragement for its future. Last, but not least here, I thank Jeffrey Haste of Deerbrook Editions for his selection of this book and the immense amount of time, energy, patience, skill and dedication that he has put in to its publication.

About the Poet

Jim Glenn Thatcher is a high school dropout with a BA in History, considerable graduate work in Modern Intellectual History, and an MFA in Creative Writing. A freelance writer with work in many papers, he was a Contributing Writer at Maine Times, the initial reviews editor at The Café Review, for two years a monthly columnist for Maine In Print (while it still *was* in print) and is currently a freelance art reviewer for The Lewiston Sun Journal. His poetry has appeared in, among others, The Puckerbrush Review, Poetry Miscellany, The Contemporary Review, Stolen Island Review, and a number of issues of both Animus and The Café Review. His chapbook "The Ur-Word" was published in 2008 by Moon Pie Press. He has been a recipient of a Martin Dibner Fellowship, a finalist for a Philip Roth writing residency at Bucknell, and a semi-finalist in both the 2014 and 2015 Paumanok Poetry competitions. Over the past seven years he has won two First Prizes for individual poems and nine Honorable Mentions (two of which were short-listed for First), all from New Millennium Writings.

Jim grew up in the only house on a dirt road in the Adirondacks, spending most of his time in what he later came to call "books, woods, and the mind" –those territories still of the greatest importance to him. A little scholar from first grade into third, he became turned off by an educational system that turns a very interesting world into a dismembered ordeal of suffering by "study." He spent the rest of those years totally infatuated with the people and places of that world, reading all that he could about it on his own. When not reading, he spent most of his time exploring the woods and mountains around him. Wanting to turn it all into a great adventure, he quit high school at the end of his junior year and joined the Army, spending most of the next three years in Germany. After that he came back home to discover that Adirondack Community College was just opening. He enrolled there and within those first few weeks experienced what he calls "a kind of conversion" back into his old-and-not-at-all-lost love of books and learning, almost instantly deciding he wanted to be a writer (he'd already thought of that) and college teacher. When he finished at Adirondack , he transferred to SUNY at New Paltz, got his degree and moved on to the graduate History program at Lehigh University.

When not in college in the years following that he drifted around, "Living the Novel" as he puts it—variously miscast as a carpenter, steel fabricator, woodworker, lineman, laborer, and factory and lumberyard hand, before at last entering Vermont College of Fine Arts to get the MFA he'd wanted for all that time—the thought of it had first come to him when he was still an undergraduate.

And now, for the last eighteen years, he has realized the goal he set for himself in his early twenties.—He is—at last—an adjunct College English Instructor—all for the love of his subjects and to honor and support his true vocation as a poet and writer. In regard to "books, woods, and the mind", he has not abandoned his studies: He still spends much of his time in the woods, and has a deep interest in the idea(s) of history, both natural and human. He currently teaches at Southern Maine Community College.

Notes

Page 47. * The epithet given by his contemporaries to Zeno of Elea (c.490-c.450 BCE), Zeno the philosopher of paradoxical mathematics. He of "the tortoise and the hare" fame, whose seemingly absurdist legacy still haunts the math texts of hapless third-graders; not to be confused with Zeno of Citium (Zeno the Stoic), toward whom I feel a certain affinity.

Page 48: *Yuan Chi (C.E.. 210-263), a scholar-poet born in Honan who rose to high office in the Wei Dynasty during the time of the wars between the Three Kingdoms. Disgusted with the stupidity and waste around him, he eventually withdrew from the court and became one of the famous group of dissolute poets known as the Seven Sages of the Bamboo Grove, noted for their impiety, drunkenness, and bitter humor.

Page 49. *Tang Dynasty, 8th Century. Li Po is one of the most famous ancient Chinese poets, known almost as much for his drunkenness as for his writing. His friend Tu Fu (see next page) also ranked highly in poetic fame, but was far more settled in his lifestyle. They were very close in spirit, but rarely together in place. Their long-lasting contacts were finally lost in the devastations of war . (See "Bittersweet," p. 51).

Page 50. *Another of the great Chinese poets. His work, too, has lasted from the Tang into the present.

Page 51.*The two friends Li Po and Tu Fu became separated by the circumstances arising from the An Lushan Rebellion, for years writing poems to each other which were never received.

Page 53: *Matsuo Bashō (1644-1694): Known for his long journeys through the still largely primitive countryside of Japan and the combined prose and poetry journals he kept of them, most notably *The Narrow Road to the Far North,* Bashō is probably the most famous Japanese poet known in the West.

Page55.*May 21, 1844-September 2, 1910. French Post-Impressionist painter in the 'Naïve' or 'Primitive' manner, known for his highly imaginative somewhat abstract works, one of which, "The Sleeping Gypsy", is a well-known example.

About the cover image

The Flammarion engraving is a wood engraving by an unknown artist, so named because its first documented appearance is in Camille Flammarion's 1888 book *L'atmosphère: météorologie populaire (The Atmosphere: Popular Meteorology)*.

This unique image was introduced for use as a cover by the author. These words: "A traveller puts his head under the edge of the firmament . . ." seem significant in the sense and importance of a poet as traveller, and as told by the author, some time passed between his first discovering it, and then finding it again near the completion of this collection.